Top Financial Mistakes to Avoid When Fixing Your Financial Situation

Samuel Dean

Why think about your financial mistakes?
Why not just pretend they didn't happen?

Because that's not how we learn. That's not how we grow. We grow by learning about mistakes and understanding how to avoid them. We grow by learning the things that work financially so that we can better our financial future. In this book we will cover the top mistakes that people make when they begin fixing their financial situation.

Misconceptions and their solutions

Mistake: Closing credit accounts immediately after they are paid off.

Closing a paid off account sounds like a smart decision a smart person would make. If you don't have the credit card, you can't use the credit card. That's simple logic. But it's wrong.

SOLUTION: Pay off the account, and DO NOT close it. Having credit available, but not making use of it, shows restraint and can improve your score. You utilized credit should remain low.

Mistake: You decide to stop contributing to a retirement account to pay off other debt faster.

While it seems to make sense to devote every dollar possible to eliminating debt today, in the long run, it's a mistake which will greatly affect your retirement income.

SOLUTION: You should contribute at least 5%-10% of your income to retirement savings as soon as you begin working and don't let eliminating debt pull any money away from that. Time is the most powerful tool in retirement savings because of compound interest. Compound interest is what gives you a solid retirement. Year after year you make more money on interest creating exponential returns. So the earlier you start contributing to a 401(k) or other retirement fund, the better off you'll be at retirement. Find other places you can cut down, like food and entertainment, in your budget to pay down credit card accounts.

Mistake: Not setting aside emergency funds for surprise expenses.

Most American consumers don't have enough cash to cover an unexpected expense of $500 or more. Imagine your washing machine breaks or worse your car hits a pothole and needs a new tire. Imagine your spouse has a car accident. What happens when your son falls out of a tree and breaks his arm? Imagine a tree falling on your house or a pipe bursting. Could you afford any of these? Or would they cripple you?

SOLUTION: Have an emergency fund! It's impossible to predict unemployment, car accidents, or cancer, which is why every home needs an emergency fund. Experts say you should put 3-6 months of expenses aside for emergencies. It might take you a while to get there if you're focused on paying off debt. This however, needs to be part of your monthly budget. You should always set aside at least 5% of your income in an emergency fund until you have 3-5 months of income set aside encase you or your spouse are out of work or in an emergency. At which point that savings can be spent on debt, investment, or fun.

Mistake: Not taking the time to verify that your credit report is correct with the credit reporting agencies.

Checking your credit report for inaccuracies is an important step in your to reducing your debt and tracking your scores upward journey. This needs to be done to ensure that you don't miss any accounts that might be almost paid off or in delinquency. It's easy to accidentally not pay off an account with less than a dollar on it and end up having late fees and missed payments added to your report.

SOLUTION: If you request one, each agency will give you a free credit. Reports from each of the major credit reporting bureaus, Equifax, Experian and TransUnion are how businesses judge your financial health when determining your credit or loan approvals. Obtain at least one every four months, from a different reporting agency each time. Check them closely for incorrect delinquencies and/or balances that hurt your credit score. This will make a difference in your ability to buy a house or car, or obtain more credit. Small inaccuracies can affect your score over drastically if not corrected in a timely manner. This also help you keep from forgetting about old accounts and ensure that they are fully paid off.

Mistake: You don't prioritize paying off your debt.

Everyone has bills and we all want to live debt free. But it's hard to not buy fun items or fancy things when we have a few extra dollars to do so. Sometimes we make a habit of this because it makes us feel good. This is bad. You must restrain yourself.

Solution: The best solution, if this is you, which it likely is, could be to consolidate your debts and make just one payment every month. Another way is give yourself x amount of fun money each month. Then never spend more than that amount on anything that is non-essential.

Mistake: Keeping Your Old Spending Habits

People are creatures of habit. We typically spend our money the same way paycheck after paycheck. You likely shop at the same stores, eat in the same restaurants and drive the same kind of cars you always have, because it's comfortable for you to continue your repetitive behaviors. This behavior is also costing you more than you can handle financially. Once you've acknowledged this you will be ready to make real changes in your life to better your financial future.

Solution: If you do not change your spending habits, you will not get out of debt. Your habits are why you are in debt in the first place.

Start with your morning habits. Do you stop for coffee every day? That could save you $5 a day alone. Bring your own lunch to work instead of eating out for lunch every day. For entertainment, go to cheaper places or if you go out for drinks often, invite your drinking group over. It's usually cheaper.

Mistake: Trying to dig your way out of debt without asking for help.

People are reluctant to ask relatives or friends for help dealing with debt for variety of reasons. Sometimes we think that being in a place of debt is shameful. Being overwhelmed with debt happens to most people at some point in their lives. It would be hard to find someone who'd never over extended themselves financially.

SOLUTION: Get some free help by calling a nonprofit credit counseling agency and talking to a counselor. Credit counselors who are trained and certified by national organizations like the National Foundation for Credit Counseling, can help save your financial future. Groups like the National Foundation for Credit Counseling can suggest the debt-relief solution that is right for you. The credit counselors will advise you on creating budgets. It's free. It'd be stupid not to take advantage of it, if you are struggling.

Mistake: Signing up for a debt-relief program without understanding what is expected of you.

It is rare to get an instant solution to any debt problems. If there is a company that promises you one, start looking elsewhere. It's likely a scam.

SOLUTION: The first thing to understand is that debt-relief programs will typically take you around 3-5 years to complete, if you follow the program to the letter. Do not expect immediate results. Instead expect slow relief. Always look into the company you choose for debt relief, find one that works for you.

The Better Business Bureau is a great place to start checking their backgrounds. Credit unions, universities and military bases should be reliable sources for recommendations of reliable debt relief organizations.

Mistake: Not creating a practical budget that you can live with forever.

It's almost impossible to have control of your finances unless you have a budget. People think it's too much work, so they don't do it. Then they have terrible finances. They wonder how they can make a great salary and still never have any money. It's because they aren't spending it wisely.

SOLUTION: Developing a realistic budget that addresses financial needs like housing, food, health care, insurance and education, but still creates room to make payments on debt can be difficult. Sometimes it makes sense to take a class or read books about budgeting. Build an amount of fun money into your budget.

Mistake: Trying to pay off multiple debts at once instead of focusing on 1 debt.

If you have multiple sources of debt it sounds like a good idea to pay them all off equally. Instead, it is smart to focus on paying them down 1 at a time. This will relieve you of the number of bills you have faster over time.

SOLUTION: Go back to your budget and focus as much money as you can at the card or account with the highest interest rate.

I hope this book was of help to you.

If you would like to learn more about budgeting you should try taking a class on Udmey.

The below hyperlinked course from Shane Kluiter that is highly rated and has over 1,000 students.

https://www.udemy.com/personal-financebudgeting-basics/learn/v4/overview

Using Code PATHTOFREEDOM you will get 50% off.

www.ingramcontent.com/pod-product-compliance
Lightning Source LLC
Chambersburg PA
CBHW031511210526
45463CB00008B/3185